A Great Idea

ENGINEERING

The Qinghai-Tibet Railway

By Sherri Devaney

NORWOODHOUSE PRESS

Cover: A train on the Qinghai-Tibet Railway leaves Lhasa headed for Beijing.

Norwood House Press
P.O. Box 316598
Chicago, Illinois 60631

For information regarding Norwood House Press, please visit our Web site at:
www.norwoodhousepress.com or call 866-565-2900.

PHOTO CREDITS: Cover: © Palani Mohan/Getty Images; © Aroon Thaewchatturat/Alamy, 12; Bow Editorial Services, 20, 26, 32; © China Photos/Getty Images, 14, 15, 19, 23, 25, 27, 38; © Colin Galloway/Alamy pg 33; © Galen Rowell/Mountain Light/Alamy, 7; © Keystone/Hulton Archive/Getty Images, 8; © Peter Parks/AFP/Getty Images, 21; Planet Observer/Universal Images Group via Getty Images, 5; © Robert Harding Picture Library Ltd/Alamy, 34; © TAO Images Limited/Alamy, 28; © Travelfile/Alamy, 11; © Wang Bo/Xinhua Press/Corbis, 37; © Wu Hong/epa/Getty Images, 41

LIBRARY OF CONGRESS CATALOGING-IN-PUBLICATION DATA

Devaney, Sherri.
  The Qinghai-Tibet Railway / by Sherri Devaney.
    pages cm -- (A great idea)
  Includes bibliographical references and index.
  Summary: "Describes the struggles and accomplishments that came with making the Qinghai-Tibet Railway the highest train line in the world. Includes glossary, websites, and bibliography for further reading"-- Provided by publisher.
  Audience: Grade 4 to 6.
  ISBN 978-1-59953-599-9 (library edition : alk. paper)
  ISBN 978-1-60357-592-8 (ebook)
  1. Qing Zang tie lu (China)--Juvenile literature. 2. Railroads--China--Tibet Autonomous Region--Design and construction--Juvenile literature. 3. Railroads--China--Qinghai Sheng--Design and construction--Juvenile literataure. 4. Railroads--China--Tibet Autonomous Region--History--Juvenile literature. 5. Railroads--China--Qinghai Sheng--History--Juvenile literature. I. Title.
  TF102.Q257D49 2013
  625.100951'5--dc23
                                                         2013012256

Manufactured in the United States of America in North Mankato, Minnesota.
257R—032014

Contents

Note: Words that are **bolded** in the text are defined in the glossary.

Chapter 1

Forging a Path to the Roof of the World

It was June 29, 2001. Nearly 1,000 people were gathered together to celebrate. Workers were about to start building a 710-mile (1,143km) railway that would connect China to its western provinces. This record-breaking railway would earn the title as the world's highest passenger train with more than 80 percent of the track 13,000 feet (3,962m) above sea level.

The railway would let millions of people get to Tibet. This is a place so remote and mysterious it was once called the Hidden Kingdom. When finished, the train would take people to Tibet's capital, **Lhasa.** Tibet is called the **Tibet Autonomous Region (TAR)**. It makes up 471,662 square miles (1.2 million square kilometers) of the southwestern part of the **People's Republic of China (PRC)**. The TAR is a bit larger than France, Germany, and Italy combined.

In this satellite photo, the dark line shows the pathway of the Qinghai-Tibet Railway. For the most part, the railway runs through the Tibetan Plateau.

The Roof of the World

In 2000 the TAR was the only part of the People's Republic of China PRC not linked to China's east via a railway. That's because Tibet is not an easy place to get to. It is a **landlocked** area. And it is almost completely surrounded by the world's largest mountains. One-third of the mountains in the world that are more than 23,000 feet (7,010m) above sea level are in Tibet. Mount Everest is the highest point on earth. It is more than 29,000 feet (8,839m) above sea level. It sits on the Tibet-**Nepal** border. Along 1,554 miles (2,501km) of Tibet's southern boundary and part of its western border are the Himalayas. The Kunlun Mountains make up Tibet's northern border. The Tanggula Mountains make up part of Tibet's border with the **Qinghai Province** to the northeast. All of these mountain ranges

A Derailed Project

There were two failed attempts at a railway to Lhasa. In 1959 workers built a rail line that started in Lanzhou, the capital city of the Gansu Province. The line went to Xining, a bustling trade city and the capital of Qinghai. The line continued another 60 miles (97km) past Xining. But then the government ran out of money. In the 1970s another attempt was made. In 1979 the railway picked up where it had left off. It reached Golmud, which was then the western frontier of central China. Again, lack of money put the train-to-Lhasa project on hold. Officials did not try again for 20 years.

have **elevations** higher than 20,000 feet (6,096m).

The TAR also sits on the world's largest and highest plateau. This is why it is often called the Roof of the World. A plateau is a flat area of land that is higher than the land around it. The altitude in the TAR can average 16,000 feet (4,877m) above sea level. The northern two-thirds of the **Tibetan Plateau** is the **Chang Tang**. According to the Wildlife Conservation Society, the Chang Tang region is "one of the last great expanses of wilderness left on Earth." The Chang Tang is home to the largest subarctic **permafrost** region in the world. This delicate frozen soil can melt. This makes traveling in the Chang Tang difficult. In some places the

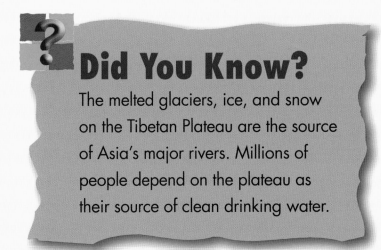

Antelope graze on the few plants that grow through the arctic permafrost in the Chang Tang region.

thawed permafrost gets so soggy it can swallow a truck. The average altitude in the Chang Tang is 15,000 feet (4,572m).

The air is very thin in Tibet. Some areas in Tibet can have nearly 50 percent less oxygen in the air than at sea level. Because the Tibetan people live in such conditions, they are not affected by the altitude. In fact, Tibetans who help Westerners climb the high mountain peaks do so without any extra oxygen. But most climbers can only climb the peaks if they breathe with oxygen tanks.

The Chinese Take Over

Tibet is very isolated. Because of this, it developed a rich and unique culture. It also kept independent from its much larger neighbor, China. But in 1949

Chinese People's Liberation Army soldiers mix cement for roads in 1951.

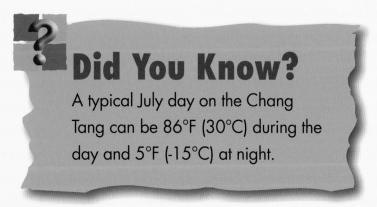

? Did You Know?

A typical July day on the Chang Tang can be 86°F (30°C) during the day and 5°F (-15°C) at night.

Chinese Communists took over the government of China. The new regime wanted to make Tibet part of China. So on September 9, 1951, China brought Tibet under its control.

Once Tibet was under Chinese control, Chinese leaders wanted a railway that let Chinese people travel to Tibet easily. They wanted Chinese people to be able to move to Tibet if they wanted to. Yet a railway seemed too hard and costly to build. Instead, they built highways into Lhasa from the east.

For three years, 100,000 Chinese and Tibetan workers moved millions of tons of earth, often by hand. They built about 400 bridges and two highways. One road went east over the mountains to Chengdu in what became the Sichuan Province. The

An Expedition with a Mission

In 1975 a young scientist named Cheng Guodong went to the Tibetan Plateau to study its permafrost. He and 20 young engineers braved the harsh terrain with small food rations. They had to constantly dig their truck out of wetlands and thawing permafrost. The group dug holes in the earth and took samples to study the layers of frozen soils. They weighed the dirt for water content. The data, carefully plotted on a map, became the first in-depth recordings of permafrost on the plateau. As a result, Cheng became one of the most well known experts on frozen soils in the world.

other road went over the Tibetan Plateau to the Qinghai Province. Thousands died during construction from hunger, altitude sickness, or exposure to the harsh winds and the cold. Before the Chinese invasion the only vehicles in Lhasa were the few that were made there. On December 15, 1954, vehicles drove into Lhasa on their own power for the first time. Tibet would never be the same.

But the highways did not make getting to Tibet from China's eastern provinces easy. People still had to take a train from **Beijing** to **Golmud** before boarding a bus to Lhasa. The trip often took more than two days. Bad weather could make the trip longer. Buses would break down. The bad road conditions often caused accidents. Trucks carrying goods slid off the badly damaged roads. Some would roll down embankments. The highways were unreliable, and their upkeep was time-consuming and costly.

Planning a Railroad

Chinese officials planned to build a railway on the plateau one day. So they sent a team of scientists to study it. One engineer, Zhang Luxin, devoted his entire career to the railway. In an interview with Abrahm Lustgarten in the latter's 2006 article, "Next Stop, Lhasa," Zhang says, "There is an ancient Chinese saying. 'I spend my whole life in one battle.'" Zhang left for Tibet right after he got married. Alone, he camped on the plateau, developed methods for building on permafrost, and planned his route. He

Before the Qinghai-Tibet Railway was built, passengers boarded buses at the Golmud Station to take them to Lhasa.

hoped that one day China could build the railway and would hire him to help.

That day would come. In 1999 President Jiang Zemin launched a plan to develop China's west area. The government again focused on building a train to Tibet. The question was, did China's engineers have the skills and technology to do it?

Zhang was determined to show the government that they were ready. He had worked for decades on the route south from Qinghai Province. This route picked up where the train from **Xining** to Golmud had left off in 1979. It would extend from Golmud to Lhasa over a naturally occurring north-south corridor.

Like other routes proposed at that time, deep gorges and glacier-topped mountain ranges had to be overcome. Still Zhang's route traveled mostly over the flat expanse of the plateau that extended for hundreds of miles. But even though the plateau was flat, it was still very high in altitude. Harsh weather and melting permafrost would make even the flat plateau a difficult route. Zhang argued it was the best route to build the railway. In fact, it had been used before for other purposes. It was the route of the Qinghai-Tibet Highway. It was also

A Natural Barrier

Writer Paul Theroux published a book in 1988 about his travels by train through China. The book was called *Riding the Iron Rooster.* When he saw the Kunlun Mountains, he thought China would never get a train over it. He wrote in his book, "The Kunlun Range is a guarantee that the railway will never get to Lhasa. That is probably a good thing. I thought I liked railways until I saw Tibet, and then I realized that I liked wilderness much more."

Writer Paul Theroux was convinced China would never get a train across the Kunlun Mountains.

the route used for the oil products pipeline built in the 1970s.

Others argued that Zhang's route was impossible. Workers could not survive the altitudes. More than 400 miles (644km) of the railway would be built on barely permanent permafrost. Some said the current technology for building on permafrost was too experimental. But Zhang convinced them that they could to do it. Officials approved the route from Golmud to Lhasa. Work began shortly thereafter. Zhang's hard work paid off.

Chapter 2

A Tough Terrain

The official groundbreaking ceremony to mark the start of construction was on June 29, 2001. But before that, survey and design teams made up of about 3,000 workers spent the spring on the plateau. They had only four months to closely examine the proposed route. So they could not afford any delays.

Altitude Sickness

Unfortunately, it was not long before thousands of them suffered from the effects of altitude sickness. They felt dizzy and nauseated. Their heads pounded. They were weak with fatigue. Others could not eat or sleep. No health-care workers on staff were able to treat them properly. People

Did You Know?

Tibet is one the few places in the world where you can get frostbite and sunburn at the same time.

A railroad worker receives treatment for mountain sickness at a construction site. The high altitudes sickened many workers and killed some.

can suffer from altitude sickness any time they are higher than 8,000 feet (2,438m). If they go up too fast, their bodies often react to the lack of oxygen.

To reverse the symptoms, they must quickly get down to a lower altitude. If they do not, they may become seriously ill. But workers on the flat expanse of the Tibetan Plateau could not do that. Descending could take them hours or days. As workers became more ill and afraid for their lives, work stopped and panic set in.

Chinese officials had to do something to calm and treat their workforce. They sent doctors able to treat altitude sickness to the camps. Officials were now aware of the crippling effects of this sickness on workers and the work schedule. They would not make the same mistake again.

Officials estimated that more than 100,000 laborers came to work in 2001. As the number of workers increased, so did the number of clinics and experienced health-care workers on hand. Eventually, thousands of medical clinics and close to 20 oxygen-making stations were set up along the lines. Oxygen was pumped into tunnels to aid workers. And effective treatment was never far away.

Facing Challenges

As workers arrived to work on the railway, they were assigned to one of the work sites scattered along the rail line. Twenty-two different railroad bureaus

Catching Your Breath

Because of the high altitudes, passenger comfort and safety had to be specially considered. The Chinese partnered with Bombardier. This is a Canadian aerospace and transportation company that built the railcars. They wanted cars that were pressurized like an airplane cabin. But that idea would not work. The train doors had to open too often. The cars would have to be re-pressurized every time the train stopped to let people off. Instead, each seat, bed, and table had an oxygen hose. Oxygen was pumped into the main cabins. This oxygen-enriched air can easily cause a fire, however. So passengers are strictly forbidden to smoke.

These passengers relax and use their cell phones even while traveling at altitudes, that, if outdoors, would leave them breathless.

worked almost independently on their piece of the project. At first, the plan was to stop working in the winter and start up again in the spring, when the weather was better. But the government wanted to keep the project moving. So it continued the railway construction through the winter.

Now workers had to deal with the harsh weather of the plateau. It gets below 32°F (0°C) there on 200 days of the year. On about 100 days of the year, windstorms and

Nearly 10,000 workers labored on the plateau under harsh conditions in December 2001.

sandstorms whip through at hurricane-force speeds. With no plants or trees on the plateau to protect them, workers were fully exposed to the weather.

Winter temperatures could dip to -22°F (-30°C). This created some technical problems. For example, pouring concrete in cold temperatures can make it less durable. **Curing** of concrete is one of the most important steps in construction. In order to cure, concrete must harden within a certain temperature range. If it is not done right, the final product will not be strong. Hardening of concrete is not a drying process. It is a chemical reaction between cement and water. This reaction is called **hydration**. If the water is too cold, this reaction stops. Then the concrete will no longer gain strength. Curing can take many days. During that time the concrete needs to stay wet and warm.

On the Move

Most vegetation cannot grow on the Tibetan Plateau because it is too cold and dry. But certain grasses grow well. Because the land cannot be used for crops, it has been used for centuries by Tibetan herders to raise livestock that feed on the grasses. Pastures feed millions of yak, sheep, and goats. These herders are called nomads because they have no permanent homes and travel from place to place. Although mobility is a key feature of their lifestyle, their movement is not random. The nomads move with the seasons and seek the best place for their animals to graze. When the nomads move on to find new pasture, they allow the land to recover and the grasses to regrow.

Now that it was winter, engineers needed to find a way to heat the water and keep the concrete warm once it was in place. They tried heating the water in huge electric boilers. This kept the mixture at 70°F (21°C). Once they poured the mixture, hot air cannons fanned the concrete until it hardened. Sometimes workers wrapped the giant pillars of bridges in blankets to keep the heat in. In the tunnels, workers forced in hot air and oxygen to keep the cement warm.

Staying on Track

With the hydration problem solved, work progressed quickly. After one year, workers had placed nearly 60 miles (97km) of track and begun work on 40 bridges and tunnels. Near Lhasa, workers started drilling a tunnel through the mountains of the Yangbajain Gorge. This would be the longest tunnel on the route.

Other tunnels being built at the same time would become record breakers. The Fenghuoshan Tunnel, between the Kunlun and Tanggula Mountains, would be 16,093 feet (4,905m) above sea level. That is more than half the cruising altitude of an airplane. It would be the highest

A watchman walks the Fenghuoshan Tunnel. At 16,093 feet above sea level it is the highest railway tunnel in the world.

tures. He was not a railway expert. He had never traveled to Tibet. He did not have any experience working in high altitudes. Despite these limitations, he was bright and willing to learn.

railway tunnel in the world. Near the Kunlun Mountain pass was another tunnel. This was the Kunlun Mountain Tunnel. It would be the longest plateau tunnel built on permafrost in the world.

In May 2002 officials hired Zhao Shiyun, a young structural engineer, to be the director. No one person at this point was overseeing the entire project. Zhao's real expertise was concrete bridge struc-

An Unpredictable Foundation

It was not long before Zhao realized what the real challenge was: the route over the permafrost. Engineers had been studying the plateau for decades. Yet a railway had never been built over such unstable and unpredictable ground at such great length or altitude. And no one was exactly sure how they were going to do it.

Permafrost is a great foundation—unless it thaws. Permafrost is ground that stays below 32°F (0°C) for more than two years. On top of permafrost is the **active layer**. This layer is not permafrost. It thaws in warm months and refreezes in cold months. In some parts of the world, like the Tibetan Plateau, the active layer can be several yards thick.

This makes a very muddy foundation in warm months.

This unpredictable active layer worried engineers. If the plateau had longer-than-normal periods of thaw, the active layer could become even deeper. This could mean even more thaw during the summer. And it could mean **frost heave** in the winter. As the ground melts then freezes

A Route That Conquers Altitude and Permafrost

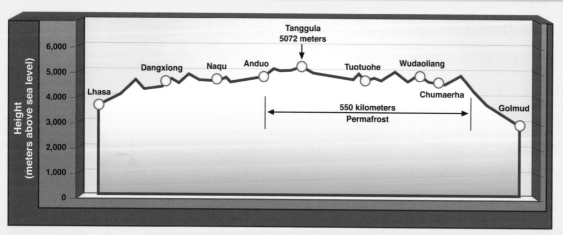

This vertical section diagram of the railroad from Lhasa to Golmud shows the altitude and permafrost locations along the route.

Three Is Better than One

Speeds of the Qinghai-Tibet Railway are 74.5 miles per hour (120kph) on the areas free of permafrost. They are 62 miles per hour (100kph) on the areas with permafrost. A special locomotive was needed to run at the high altitudes of the railway. General Electric is an American company. It designed and built the three diesel-powered 3,800 horsepower engines that were made to pull the train in high altitudes. At the last leg of the journey from Golmud to Lhasa, rail staff switch from one regular locomotive to the three specially designed engines. This helps in the final climb toward the Tanggula Pass.

This General Electric locomotive was specially built to run at higher altitudes.

again, it contracts and then expands. This can place enormous stress on the foundation of the railway above it. It can cause the railway to turn or buckle in ways that look like a roller coaster's twisting track.

In severe cases, permafrost can melt. This happens if the temperature of the ground below the surface of the permafrost rises above 30°F (-1°C). The Tibetan Plateau is not like places in Alaska and Siberia. There consistently freezing temperatures keep permafrost from thawing. In fact, the Tibetan Plateau is just a few degrees from turning into mud.

Chapter 3

Keeping It Cool

The unstable permafrost was clearly the biggest challenge yet. Construction would make the permafrost even more fragile. This is because it can speed up thawing or cause it to thaw in new places. The only chance engineers had to keep the railway intact was to manage Mother Nature in order to keep the ground cool.

Engineering Solutions

Engineers wanted to make sure the tracks stayed straight and the foundation stable. They needed to prevent structural damage from thawing permafrost. So they used many methods to stabilize ground temperatures on the train route. The Tibetan Plateau has a low latitude and high elevation. So the sun beats down on it. Engineers decided to use metal shades to keep the ground from absorbing heat. In spots with the strongest sun, workers put up metal sun shades along the tracks.

Engineers also used methods to keep the ground cold or make it colder. They needed to remove heat from the embankment. One way they did this was to use **convection** in the form of crushed rock. They put down a 2- to 3-foot (61cm to 81cm) layer of loose, medium-size rocks under the embankments. As warm air rises, the space between the rocks gives it somewhere to go. The idea was that the spaces between the rocks would allow air to flow freely and keep the ground cool.

By using materials that let air flow, engineers created insulation between the

Workers straighten track along the railway. The layer of loose rock that keeps the permafrost cool can also be seen.

A Hollow Solution

Engineers used another way to keep the rail bed frozen. They put in hollow concrete pipes beneath the tracks. These pipes allowed air to pass through the embankment center and draw out heat from the soil. One problem with this method is that in the summer, warm air flows through the pipes. This increases heat absorption in the embankment. That's why these systems need shutters. These allow the pipes to be sealed during warm months.

cools the permafrost below. This method was not new. But it was the first time it was used as the main solution and on such a large scale. Engineers also raised the railway embankment between 7 and 33 feet (2m and 10m). This insulated the ground from the heat made by the tracks.

Another cooling method, and a much more costly one, was **thermosyphons**, or cooling sticks. Each stick was a pressurized vertical tube about 35 feet (10.7m) deep and 8 inches (20cm) in diameter. Ammonia, a liquid with a low boiling point, was poured into the bottom. The sticks were placed into the ground along the railway. As air temperature drops below that of the embankment, the tubes use evaporation and condensation of the liquid to remove heat from the

frozen ground and the road above it. This lowers the heat intake by the soil during warmer months. It also promotes heat loss in the winter. So it both insulates and

embankment and spread it into the atmosphere. This left the earth cooler. In an area of unstable permafrost like the plateau, thermosyphons stabilize and refreeze soil that has thawed.

As the director of the project, Zhao Shiyun knew that no matter what cooling

Did You Know?
Permafrost acts like a waterproof barrier. This lets ponds, lakes, and marshes important to plants and animals develop in the summer. Without permafrost, water would soak in or run off the land. And the region would become very dry.

Workers rest on concrete pipes to be used as thermosyphons along the railway. The pipes use condensation and evaporation of liquid to remove heat from the embankment.

precautions were taken, some parts of the plateau were just too fragile to put railway tracks across. The safe thing to do was leap over these areas with bridges. The original plan included bridges. But Zhao and his team wanted another 60 miles (97km) of them. They wanted 105 miles (169km) of bridges in total. Towers to support the bridges would be placed deep in frozen ground. This method was by far the most costly. It is used by engineers only as a last resort.

Tracks and Tunnels

Construction moved forward at a frantic pace. Workers finished the tracks from Golmud up the Kunlun Mountains. By April 2003 a locomotive traveled through the finished tunnel through these mountains. The train carried its own premade tracks on its freight cars ready to be installed on the plateau. These tracks were 75 feet (23m) long and looked like ladders. Already attached to concrete cross ties, they were ready to be put in place on the plateau. The Chinese built a machine called the PG30 to install these tracks. The PG30 grabbed sections of track and dropped them in place. After

it put down the rails, it would roll over them and start again. This method allowed workers to install nearly 2 miles (3.2km) of track per day. Another similar machine put up pre-made sections of bridges after the pylons were in place. By May 2003 the railway was just past the Kunlun Pass and at an altitude of 15,000 feet (4,572m).

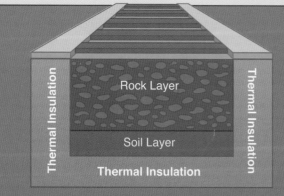

Roadbed Insulation

Thermal Insulation

Rock Layer

Thermal Insulation

Soil Layer

Thermal Insulation

A cutaway view of the railway roadbed shows the layer of thermal insulation material that was then filled with a layer of soil and a layer of crushed rock to keep the surrounding permafrost from melting.

A PG30 locomotive moves a 75-foot (23m) premade track into place along the railway. Using the PG30 allowed workers to lay 2 miles (3.2km) of new track a day.

At this time officials and engineers chose a part of the ridge of the Tanggula Pass that separated Qinghai from the TAR as the location for the highest train stop on the route and in the world. In July 2003 they chose a farming village named N'eu as the final stop on the route. This village is 9 miles (14.5km) south of Lhasa. It would be the home of the new $35 million train station. September 2003 brought another milestone. Workers broke through the end of the long tunnel begun in 2001 at the Yangbajain Gorge. It was the second-longest tunnel on the route. It bore through 2 miles (3.2km) of mountainside.

A Faster Pace

That winter Chinese officials pushed the deadline up one year. They wanted trains in service by early 2006, a full year ahead

? Did You Know?

Tibet is often called the world's third pole because it has the biggest ice fields outside of the Arctic and Antarctic.

needed for the project, progress was at the mercy of the pace of the PG30.

Zhao and his team had a brainstorm. If they started a railway inside the TAR on the other side of the permafrost region, they would be able to install tracks and bridges at different points. They chose Amdo, a town just inside the TAR border, to be a production station for premade materials.

There was still one big problem. They would need to use the PG30 to lay the

of the original deadline. There was still 550 miles (885km) of track to install. Even if they could get all the supplies

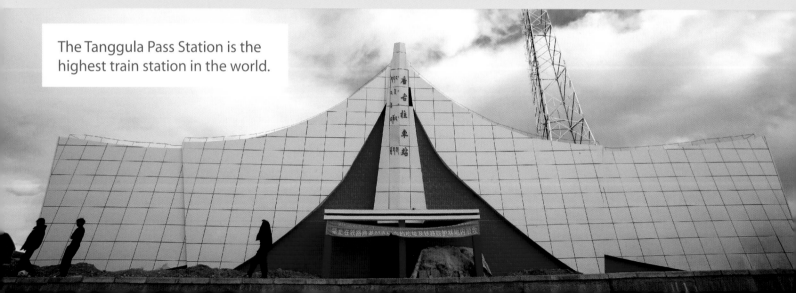

The Tanggula Pass Station is the highest train station in the world.

A Scar on the Landscape

On November 14, 2001, there was an 8.1 magnitude earthquake in China. It caused a 267-mile (430km) surface rupture on the Kunlun fault. Luckily, railway construction had just started, so there was not too much damage. For passenger safety, engineers made sure not to build bridges, tunnels, or stations on active faults. Then they put steel reinforcement bars on these main structures. The bars keep the concrete from cracking in the event of another earthquake. It would be too costly to put such reinforcements on the entire railway. So engineers installed earthquake-detection systems instead.

track and the bridge-building erector to install the bridges. This machinery was twice the size and weight of a locomotive. The only way to get it to Amdo was to take it apart, put it on a truck, and transport it on a highway.

But years of harsh weather and heaving permafrost had damaged the highway. In some places it had collapsed. Workers now had to rebuild the road and bridges from the end of the existing tracks in Wudaoliang to Amdo.

By the late spring of 2004, workers had finished the highway. Diesel rigs weighted down with the heavy load slowly and carefully transported the vital machinery to Amdo. The convoys of heavy machinery put the roads to the test, but they held up.

A Risky Endeavor

According to Abrahm Lustgarten in his book *China's Great Train*, engineers had planned to use the newest German-built boring machines instead of human labor when they began the 2-mile-long (3.2km) tunnel at the Yangbajain Gorge. Tunnel boring was very dangerous. Many lives were lost while building railway tunnels in the 1970s. But the machines could not be transported to the location of the tunnel. Without modern machines to drill holes in the bedrock, workers were forced to do it the old-fashioned way. They had to do it by hand. Workers would drill holes into bedrock or ice. They packed the holes with explosives. Then they ran to escape the blast.

That summer work on the railway raced to completion from three points: Amdo to Lhasa and from both ends of the Amdo to Wudaoliang route.

Reaching a Milestone

In June 2004 the first section of rails was dropped into place in Amdo. A ceremony with 2,000 workers marked the event. A railway was finally in the TAR 250 miles (410km) from Lhasa. The line soon reached another 85 miles (137km) to Nagqu. This was the commercial center of the northern TAR. Years later it would be the site of many mining exploration projects. Track laying toward Lhasa moved quickly and smoothly.

The project moved quickly with workers on the job around the clock. By April 3, 2005, tracks from Amdo were only 100 miles (161km) from Lhasa. More than three months later, the project was 90 percent completed. By October 2005 the railway to Tibet, or as many called it, the "Sky Train," was done.

Chapter 4

Ready or Not, Here They Come

It was July 1, 2006, only five years after construction had begun. The first train carrying 600 passengers left Golmud Station traveling south. Thirteen hours later the train from Golmud reached Lhasa.

Today the average trip from Beijing to Lhasa takes 47 hours and 28 minutes. It travels a distance of 2,025 miles (3,259km). Of this, 710 miles (1,143km) is the new section from Golmud to Lhasa. This part has nine viewing platforms set up along the way.

A Ride to the Sky

Passengers ride in the steel bubble of the specially designed train. There they feel protected from the sand and harsh weather on the plateau. About 99 miles (159km) after leaving Golmud, the train goes through its first pass. This is the Kunlun Mountain pass. Here the altitude rises sharply from 9,186 feet to 15,420 feet (2,800m to 4,700m). Passengers see a quick change from hot summer to severe winter. There

Qinghai-Tibet Railway

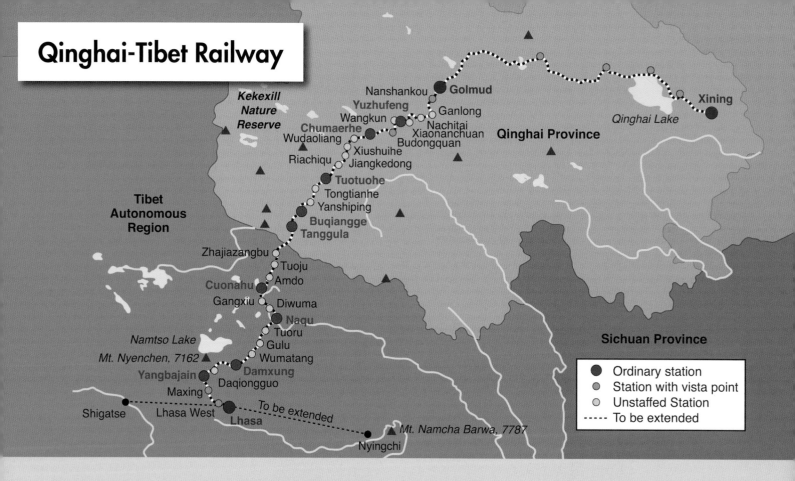

Kekexill Nature Reserve

Nanshankou · **Golmud**
Yuzhufeng · Ganlong
Wangkun · Nachitai
Chumaerhe · Xiaonanchuan
Wudaoliang · Budongquan
Xiushuihe
Riachiqu · Jiangkedong
Tuotuohe
Tongtianhe
Yanshiping
Buqiangge
Tanggula

Xining
Qinghai Lake
Qinghai Province

Tibet Autonomous Region

Zhajiazangbu
Tuoju
Amdo
Cuonahu
Gangxiu · Diwuma
Naqu
Tuoru
Gulu
Namtso Lake · Wumatang
Mt. Nyenchen, 7162
Yangbajain
Maxing · Daqiongguo
Damxung
Shigatse · Lhasa West · To be extended
Lhasa
Nyingchi · Mt. Namcha Barwa, 7787

Sichuan Province

- ⬤ Ordinary station
- ⬤ Station with vista point
- ○ Unstaffed Station
- ---- To be extended

are also snow-covered mountain peaks. Although this pass may seem like the top of the world, the train will go over an even higher elevation. This is the Tanggula Mountain pass. It is the natural boundary between Qinghai and Tibet.

At this pass, which is a 3-mile (4.8km) climb into the sky, passengers may find themselves at the highest elevations of their lives: 16,640 feet (5,072m). Here the station stands alone. There are no other signs of civilization around it. The world thought China could not build a railway over this hurdle. But it did. Many passengers have medicines that fight altitude sickness, and the special railway cars are pumped with

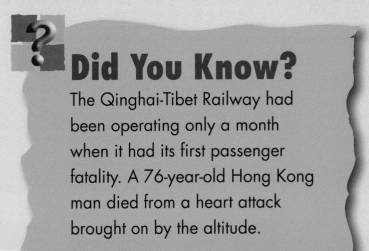

A Lhasa-bound train tops the Kunlun Pass at 15,420 feet (4,700m) in specially designed cars that protect passengers from harsh weather on the plateau.

oxygen. But many people still report feeling nauseated, dizzy, and euphoric at this pass. Some even report hallucinations. From there, the train descends into Amdo and then Nagqu. In Lhasa passengers get off at the Lhasa station.

The Land of Opportunity

In 2007, the year after the railway opened to regular passenger service, 4 million tourists entered Tibet. According to the Qinghai-Tibet Railway Company, the number of passengers in 2012 reached

The Lhasa Station at Lhasa. Millions of travelers pass through Lhasa via the railway each year.

Know the Risks

Before boarding the train to Lhasa, passengers must fill out a passenger health registration card. The card is given out when tickets are purchased. Passengers must read the warnings about high-altitude travel. Then they must sign the card before they are allowed to board the train.

10.76 million. Han Chinese (China's ethnic majority) workers, investors, merchants, and soldiers arrived in droves. Officials promised to increase tourism by 2020 to 20 million visitors a year.

To make room for all of these new tourists, Lhasa changed a lot. Thousands of stores and restaurants were built. Hundreds of new hotels were also built. Traffic in parts of Lhasa exploded. New businesses sprang up all over the TAR.

Tibetans and their supporters believe the real reason for the train was better access to the TARs mineral resources. China had nearly 1,000 geographers scope out the area before the Golmud-to-Lhasa line was built. Soon after riders boarded the new line, China announced their findings. They found several billion tons of iron ore. There were 30 million to 40 million tons (27 million t to 36 million t) of copper. And there were 40 million tons (36.8 t) of lead and zinc.

Having such a large supply of resources could help China support its huge growth. It could change China's reliance on imports of copper and iron. China needs iron for its steel mills and construction and auto industries. It uses copper to make communications and electronic products. Copper is in very short supply in China. But now the railway has brought it within reach. Tibet's supporters believe that Tibet will not benefit from these discoveries. They believe Tibet will have a surge of immigrants, depletion of their resources, and pollution of their land.

In addition to greater access to minerals, the railway provides access to many rivers and mountain gorges. These can be sources of electrical power. It is also easier for the government to access oil and natural gas fields in northern Tibet and Qinghai. Tibet's supporters fear that these industries will cause pollution, oil spills, and chemical-waste dumping.

But some people believe that the new railway will bring opportunities to the youth of Tibet. John Makin, a visiting scholar at the American Enterprise Institute, wrote an article in 2007 called

The railway allowed the Chinese to build oil fields like these in Tibet.

A Migration Illusion

The Tibetan antelope is an endangered species. The railway cuts through its migration path. To avoid disturbing its path, 33 overpasses were built for it to migrate under. In an effort to show people that this was working, a picture of dozens of antelope migrating peacefully under the overpasses with the train passing behind them was released to the press. The picture won many awards. It was not long, however, before savvy Internet users figured out that the picture was a fake. The photographer used a Photoshop trick to blend two different pictures.

Engineers built overpasses and fences to keep endangered Tibetan antelope off railway tracks and redirect their migratory routes.

"The Lhasa Frontier." In it he said, "The outlook for traditionalists is bleak, but for most Tibetans, the chances for a better future are enhanced by the construction of the rail line to Lhasa."

Threats to the Future of the Railway

It is not just Tibet's future that concerns people. They are also worried about the future of the railway. Soon after the Golmud-to-Lhasa part of the railway was complete, China's Ministry of Railways spokesman Wang Yongping said that the foundation was sinking and cracking in some places. Some engineers said that the cracks were expected signs of recovery from the disturbance of the construction. Despite the cause, engineers knew that such a long railway built on permafrost would have to be watched and maintained constantly. But what if the ground was warming faster than engineers thought it would?

Climate change poses the biggest threat to the future of the railway. Changes in climate are different than changes in weather. *Weather* refers to conditions over a short time. *Climate* refers to conditions over a very long time. If climate in an area changes, so will the state of its frozen ground.

The National Snow and Ice Data Center (NSDIC) says the active layer (that melts in summer) on the Tibetan Plateau has become 40 inches (102cm) thicker in the last 50 years. As it becomes thicker, the permafrost layer becomes thinner.

If the earth's climate, and with it the Tibetan Plateau, warms, the active layer would get even thicker. **Taliks** would form. These are layers or bodies of unfrozen ground in a permafrost area. If this process continues, no permafrost could be left at all. Thawing permafrost can alter a landscape a lot. Tingjun Zhang, a senior research scientist at the NSDIC, explains:

Permafrost is degrading quickly all around the world. It's happening faster than we thought. . . . Without permafrost in a region, ecosystems will change completely. Carbon can also be released from permafrost into the atmosphere, which could accelerate global warming.

. . . Changes in permafrost will have serious impacts. . . . For example, bridges may collapse, highways may become damaged, and railroads may not work.

Those who planned the Qinghai-Tibet railway did expect some effects from climate change. To balance these effects, they used their cooling methods. And some of these methods have worked. For example, one study showed that the crushed-stones method worked. It kept the ground up to 35°F (19.6°C) cooler. In some places the permafrost even increased.

But when the railway was planned in 2001, it was designed to withstand an air temperature increase of 33°F (18.5°C) over the next 50 years. Experts now think that

Workers construct a bridge on the new rail extension to the foot of Mt. Everest.

Damaging Rays

Just like airplane windows, passenger train windows on the Qinghai-Tibet railway are made to block out solar radiation. For roughly every 320-foot (98m) increase in altitude, ultraviolet (UV) levels increase 10 to 12 percent. That is because at higher elevations, the atmosphere filters out less radiation. Exposure to UV radiation can cause diseases like cataracts. This is a disease of the lenses of the eyes. Snow cover on the plateau adds to the problem. Snow can reflect as much as 80 percent of UV radiation. This means a person gets hit by the same rays twice.

temperatures may rise higher. Scientists like Cheng Guodong are not too worried. He believes they will adapt the railways to rising temperatures.

Railway Extensions

In fact, the Chinese have so much faith in the Golmud to Lhasa line that they are connecting more of China with it. Since the Qinghai-Tibet Railway was finished in 2005, China has increased passenger services from major eastern cities. Seven major cities now have trains bound for Lhasa.

There are also plans to extend the railway into other remote areas of Tibet. A $2 billion project will connect Lhasa with Shigatse. Shigatse is located to the southwest of Lhasa. It lies at the foot of Mount Everest. It also borders China's neighbors: India, Nepal, and Bhutan. The railway will be 157 miles (253km) long and is expected to be finished by 2015. Another line will connect Lhasa to

Nyingchi in the southeastern part of Tibet. China expects the lines to further increase trade and development in the TAR.

The railway and the permafrost beneath and around it are constantly watched. How the railway is maintained under the challenges of a changing climate system will give useful information to scientists and engineers worldwide. As Stuart A. Harris explains in the 2011 book *Engineering Earth: The Impacts of Megaengineering Projects*, "From an international point of view, the railroad represents an important milestone in the development of methods of construction on warm permafrost." The politics and stability of the railway are uncertain. But most agree that the Qinghai-Tibet Railway is a modern engineering marvel.

Glossary

active layer [AK-tiv LAY-er]: In places with permafrost, this is the top layer of soil that thaws during the summer and freezes again during the autumn.

Beijing [BEY-jeeng]: The capital of China, located in the northeastern part of the country.

Chang Tang [chang thang]: This region stretches west to east across the northern two-thirds of the Tibetan Plateau. It has an average altitude of 15,000 feet (4572m). The area consists of rolling grassland broken by hills, glacier-capped mountains, and large basins of wetlands and lakes. The land is too cold to support forests or agriculture.

climate change [KLY-mit change]: Changes in climate on many different time scales, from decades to millions of years, and the possible causes of such changes.

convection [kon-VEK-shun]: The movement caused within a fluid by the tendency of hotter and therefore less dense material to rise, and colder, denser material to sink under the influence of gravity, which results in transfer of heat.

curing [KYOOR-ing]: The process of maintaining a certain moisture and temperature for freshly placed concrete for some specified time for proper hardening of the concrete.

elevations [el-uh-VAY-shuns]: The vertical distances between a reference point, such as sea level, and the top of an object or point on Earth, such as a mountain.

frost heave [FRAWST heev]: The uplift of soil or other surface deposits that are due to expansion of groundwater when it freezes.

Golmud [GEER-mu]: A city in the central Qinghai Province in western China. Golmud stands at the intersection of two ancient routes that have become highways. It is connected to the national rail network via Lanzhou, and in 2006 southward to Lhasa. Because of its alpine plains at 7,000 to 9,000 feet (2,134m to 2,743m), it was unwelcoming to most lowlander Chinese.

hydration [high-DRAY-shun]: The chemical reaction that begins once water is combined with cement. The curing process relies on the maintenance of the hydration reaction.

landlocked [land-lokt]: Completely surrounded by land with no access to the sea.

Lhasa [LAH-suh]: The capital of the TAR. It is located at an elevation of nearly 12,000 feet (3,658m) in the Tibetan Himalayas. It has served as the religious center of Tibet since at least the ninth century.

Nepal [NAY-pawl]: A country of central Asia in the Himalayas between India and southwest China. Katmandu is the capital and the largest city.

People's Republic of China (PRC) [PEE-pulz ree-PUB-lik of CHI-nah]: A Communist nation that covers a vast territory in eastern Asia. It is the world's most populous country, with a population of over 1.3 billion.

permafrost [PUR-muh-frawst]: A layer of soil or bedrock that has been continuously frozen for at least two years. It is found throughout most of the polar regions and underlies about one-fifth of the earth's land surface.

Qinghai Province [CHING-hahy PRAH-vince]: A province in northwestern China. It is bordered by Gansu and Sichuan Provinces and the TAR. The capital is Xining. It forms the northeastern part of the Tibetan Plateau and is mostly above 13,000 feet (3,962m) in elevation.

taliks [TA-leeks]: Areas of unfrozen ground surrounded by permafrost.

Tibet Autonomous Region (TAR) [ti-BET aw-TAWN-uh-muhs REE-juhn]: Tibet's official name since 1965 when China set up autonomous regions, prefectures, and counties in places that had one ethnic majority in the population. It is 471,662 square miles (1.2 million square kilometers) of the southwestern part of the PRC.

Tibetan Plateau [ti-Bet-in plah-TOE]: The largest plateau in the world, located in central Asia.

thermosyphons [THUR-muh-sigh-fuhnz]: Tubes that contain a chemical that transfers heat from the soils underneath up to the surface of the road.

Xining [SHE-ning]: A city of central China north-northeast of Chengdu. It is the capital of Qinghai Province and was long a commercial center on the caravan route to Tibet.

Books

Jacqueline Briggs Martin, *The Chiru of High Tibet: A True Story*. New York: Houghton Mifflin Books for Children, September 27, 2010.

Thomas J. Csordas. Boy on the Lion Throne: The Childhood of the 14th Dalai Lama. New York: Flash Point, an imprint of Roaring Book Press, 2009.

Peter Sis, *Tibet Through the Red Box*. New York: Farrar, Straus and Giroux, 1998.

Websites

China Tibet Train www.chinatibettrain.com. This site provides information about the train's schedules, routes, and fares. It also has facts about Tibet, including its climate, geography, and people. It lists the nine platforms from which passengers can view scenery, as well as photographs from these stations. It also describes the ticket classes and the facilities on board.

National Snow and Ice Data Center (NSIDC) http://nsidc.org. This site supports research and provides information about the world's frozen realms: the snow, ice, glaciers, frozen ground, and climate interactions that make up earth's cryosphere. The site provides information on permafrost and the effects of climate change and global warming on permafrost degradation. Contains information and educational activities on permafrost for grades 5 through 8.

Tibet Post www.tibetpost.com. The Tibet Post is a Tibetan news service based in Dharamshala, northern India. It was formed in March 2008 by a group of young Tibetan journalists eager to promote democracy through freedom of expression in Tibetan communities. The Tibet Post closely follows developments inside Tibet and the activities and workings of Tibetans in exile.

Index

About the Author

Sherri Devaney is a writer and editor devoted to challenging and inspirational topics for students, including health and wellness, engineering, and the environment. She lives in New Jersey with her husband and two sons, Sean and Jeremy, and their beagle, Scout.